THE ULTIMATE MARGARITA COOKBOOK

100 MARGARITA COCKTAILS AND MARGARITA-INFUSED FOODS

SKYLAR DAVES

All rights reserved.

Disclaimer

The information contained in this eBook is meant to serve as a comprehensive collection of strategies that the author of this eBook has done research about. Summaries, strategies, tips and tricks are only recommendation by the author, and reading this eBook will not guarantee that one's results will exactly mirror the author's results. The author of the eBook has made all reasonable effort to provide current and accurate information for the readers of the eBook. The author and its associates will not be held liable for any unintentional error or omissions that may be found. The material in the eBook may include information by third parties. Third party materials comprise of opinions expressed by their owners. As such, the author of the eBook does not assume responsibility or liability for any third party material or opinions. Whether because of the progression of the internet, or the unforeseen changes in company policy and editorial submission guidelines, what is stated as fact at the time of this writing may become outdated or inapplicable later.

The eBook is copyright © 2022 with all rights reserved. It is illegal to redistribute, copy, or create derivative work from this eBook whole or in part. No parts of this report may be reproduced or retransmitted in any reproduced or retransmitted in any forms whatsoever without the writing expressed and signed permission from the author.

TABLE OF CONTENTS

TABLE OF CONTENTS 4
INTRODUCTION 8
MARGARITA-INFUSED DISHES 9
   1. Barbecued fish margarita 10
   2. Charred Margarita beef medallions 13
   3. Chicken margarita 17
   4. Ensalada de margarita 20
   5. Grilled grouper margarita 23
   6. Margarita beef with orange salsa 26
   7. Margarita shrimp with fettuccine 29
   8. Margarita steaks 33
   9. Margarita's pasta primavera 36
   10. Shark margarita 39
   11. Beef and tequila stew 42
   12. Broiled chicken with tequila and lime 45
   13. Honey-lime-tequila chicken 48
   14. Pan-seared salmon 50
   15. Pasta with tequila, avocado and shrimp 54
   16. Yellowtail snapper with mango 57
   17. Tequila-orange chicken 61
   18. Tequila-lime shrimp 64
   19. Tequila pasta Quattro fromaggio 67
   20. Sweet corn, jicama salad with tequila 70
   21. Pork tenderloin in tequila 73
   22. Chickens marinated in margarita 76
   23. Santa Fe shrimp with tequila sauce 79
   24. Sweet potato and Tequila soup 82

MARGARITA DESSERTS 85

25. Margarita pie 86
26. Frozen strawberry margarita dessert 88
27. Frozen strawberry margarita pie 91
28. Mango key lime margaritas 94
29. Margarita cheesecake 96
30. Margarita pot de crème 100
31. Strawberry margarita mousse 103
32. Margarita fruit salad 106
33. Spanish almond cake laced with tequila 109
34. Strawberries bowl with tequila 113
35. Lentil cakes with nopalito cactus salsa 115
36. Tequila spiked watermelon soup 118
37. Corn crab cakes with margarita butter 122

MARGARITA CONDIMENTS 125

38. Grapefruit margarita sauce 126
39. Monterey jack tequila fondue 129
40. Margarita glaze for poultry 131
41. Margarita jalapeno salsa 133
42. Margarita marinade 135
43. Margarita brine 137
44. Margarita shrimp marinade 139
45. Tequila lime relish 141

MARGARITA APPETIZERS 143

46. Margarita balls 144
47. Margarita muffins 148
48. Margarita pork kabobs 151
49. Margarita shrimp and vegetable kabobs 154
50. Margarita shrimp skewers 157
51. Margarita shrimp tacos 161
52. Fajitas served with a tequila sunrise 165

53. Gala nachos with mango-tequila sauce........... 170
54. Lime and tequila sweet potatoes...................... 173
55. Grilled tequila lime pineapple chunks............... 175

CLASSIC MARGARITA COCKTAILS....................178

56. Apricot margaritas.. 179
57. Beer margarita.. 182
58. Blue margarita... 184
59. Cactus pear margaritas................................... 186
60. Cafe margaritas... 188
61. Fresh lime margaritas..................................... 191
62. Frothy margarita.. 194
63. Frozen mango margarita................................. 196
64. Frozen melon margaritas................................. 199
65. Jalapeno margaritas.. 201
66. Margarita granita... 203
67. Papaya margarita.. 206
68. Raspberry margarita....................................... 209
69. Watermelon margarita..................................... 211
70. Yucatin margaritas with fruit........................... 213
71. Beer margarita.. 216
72. Margarita liqueur... 218
73. Iced margarita... 220
74. Green Margarita.. 222

MODERN MARGARITA COCKTAILS................... 225

75. Casa Ginger Mint Paloma................................ 226
76. Oaxacan Old Fashioned.................................. 228
77. The Marble Queen... 230
78. Milagro Mexican Martini................................... 232
79. El Gavilan.. 234
80. It's Greek to Me... 236
81. Blue-cumber Lime Margarita........................... 238

82.	MANHATTAN GOES HOLLYWOOD	240
83.	THE MYSTIC MARVEL	242
84.	ROSEMARY MARGARITA	244
85.	BACCARAT ROUGE	246
86.	BLOOD ORANGE MARGARITA	248
87.	SOMETHING WICKED	250
88.	THE BLUEBONNET	253
89.	TEQUILA'S NEW FASHION	255
90.	GHOST PEPPER MARGARITA	257
91.	MOURNING DOVES	259
92.	SMOKEY ARROYO	261
93.	TEPACHE KID	263
94.	SMOKIN' MARGARITA	265
95.	VAMPIRO	267
96.	CHAI MEZCALITA	269
97.	HIBISCUS SMASH	272
98.	DEVIL'S MARGARITA	274
99.	BLOODY MARIA	276
100.	YUCATIN MARGARITAS WITH FRUIT	278

CONCLUSION..........281

INTRODUCTION

A margarita is a cocktail consisting of tequila, orange liqueur, and lime juice often served with salt on the rim of the glass. The drink is served shaken with ice, blended with ice or without ice. Although it has become acceptable to serve a margarita in a wide variety of glass types, ranging from cocktail and wine glasses to pint glasses and even large schooners, the drink is traditionally served in the eponymous margarita glass, a stepped-diameter variant of a cocktail glass or champagne coupe.

There are hundreds of permutations of margaritas. Margaritas can be churned out in every conceivable flavor from pomegranate to strawberry, raspberry, ginger-pineapple, cucumber mint, green tea, and chocolate. Margarita can also be infused into dishes like Chicken Margarita or Appetizers like Shrimp Skewers!

MARGARITA-INFUSED DISHES

1. Barbecued fish margarita

Yield: 4 Servings

Ingredient

- 1½ pounds Fish fillets (your choice)
- ⅓ cup Tequila, white or gold
- ½ cup Tripple sec
- ¾ cup Lime juice
- 1 teaspoon Salt
- 2½ Garlic cloves, crushed
- 1 tablespoon Vegetable oil
- 3 Tomatoes, medium, diced
- 1 Onion, finely chopped
- 1 tablespoon Jalapenos, minced
- 2 tablespoons Cilantro, fresh, chopped
- 1 pinch Sugar
- 1 Pepper

Directions:

a) Place fish in a non-aluminum dish large enough to hold it in a single layer.

b) Combine tequila, triple sec, lime juice, salt, garlic, and 2t oil and pour over the fish, rubbing all over. Cover and marinate for ½ hour at room temperature or up to 3 hours in the refrigerator, turning occasionally. Just before serving, combine tomatoes, onions, chilies, cilantro, sugar and salt to taste. Heat the grill to VERY hot.

c) Remove fish from marinade, pat dry (reserving marinade) and brush lightly with 1 t oil and grind pepper over the surface. Cook on a greased grill for about 4 minutes per side, or until flesh is opaque.

d) Meanwhile, boil marinade in a saucepan for 2 minutes, remove and discard garlic cloves, and spoon a little over the fish. Spoon the tomato salsa alongside and serve.

2. Charred Margarita beef medallions

Yield: 4 Servings

Ingredient

- 1 tablespoon Olive oil
- 1 tablespoon Unsalted butter
- 1½ pounds Tenderloin of beef; cut in 1" thick medallions
- Salt and pepper; to taste
- 1 small Vidalia onion; cut in medium dice
- 2 Poblano peppers; washed, seeded and cut in medium dice
- 1 tablespoon Toasted and ground cumin seed
- 2 ounces Gold tequila
- ¼ cup Lime juice
- 1 cup Rich veal stock
- 2 ounces Orange liquor
- 1 tablespoon Orange zest

- ½ cup Heavy cream
- ½ teaspoon Salt
- ½ teaspoon Ground black pepper

Directions:

a) Heat the olive oil and butter in a sauté pan over medium heat, season the beef medallions with salt and pepper, and add to the hot pan.

b) Turn the heat up to high and char both sides of the beef well. To keep the beef rare to medium rare, cook quickly, turning once only after the beef has browned on the first side. Remove the beef from the pan, place on a warm platter, and set aside. Add the diced onions and poblano peppers to the sauté pan, evenly spread out and cook till wilted.

c) Add the cumin and combine well to toast the spice again. Working carefully away from the flame, add the tequila to the pan, deglaze the pan by swirling the tequila and set back over low heat to reduce. Add the lime juice and reduce to almost dry before adding the veal stock.

d) Reduce the stock by half over high heat and add the orange liquor and fresh orange zest.

e) Cook for 2 minutes and then add the heavy cream. Do not allow to boil but gently simmer for 2 minutes before adding the salt and pepper. Serve the beef on a bed of sauce with corn pudding on the side.

3. Chicken margarita

Yield: 4 servings

Ingredient

- 3 (to 3.5 lb.) fresh frying chicken
- 1 tablespoon Ground cumin
- 1 tablespoon Chile powder
- Juice of three limes
- 10 Cloves fresh garlic, finely chopped
- 3 tablespoons Olive oil
- ½ cup Tequila (white or gold)
- ½ cup Water
- 1 Bunch fresh cilantro for garnish

Directions:

a) Cut the chicken into serving pieces and remove skin.

b) In a bowl, combine cumin, chile powder, lime juice, garlic and 1 Tablespoons of the olive oil. Marinate chicken in this mixture for 20 minutes.

c) In a heavy skillet, heat remaining oil, brown chicken pieces on all sides.

d) Add marinade, tequila and water. Cover pan and poach gently until chicken is cooked through, about 25 minutes.

e) Transfer chicken pieces to a platter. Reduce sauce over high heat until of a good consistency and pour over chicken. Garnish with cilantro leaves. 4 servings.

4. Ensalada de margarita

Yield: 4 Servings

Ingredient

- ½ Fresh pineapple
- 2 Grapefruits
- 4 Orange
- 1 Avocado
- 1 slice Watermelon; cut into wedges
- 1 cup Sliced almonds
- Lettuce greens; washed and chilled
- 1 cup Pineapple juice
- 3 tablespoons Lime juice; fresh
- ⅓ cup White Tequila
- ½ teaspoon Powdered sugar and salt
- 2 tablespoons Olive oil

Directions:

a) Mix all Ingredients for the dressing. Shake in a jar and chill. Using just the meat of the pineapple, cut into 1" cubes. Peel the grapefruits, oranges and avocado. Cut into 1" cubes (the avocado should be $\frac{1}{2}$"). Toss together with the dressing.

b) Place the lettuce greens fanned out on a plate. Place fruit mixture on greens, top with sliced almonds and garnish with water melon wedges. Serve chilled on a chilled plate. This would make a refreshing summer lunch dish.

5. Grilled grouper margarita

Yield: 1 servings

Ingredient

- 1½ pounds Grouper fillets
- ½ cup Triple sec
- 1 teaspoon Salt plus more to taste
- 1 tablespoon Vegetable oil
- 1 medium Onion, finely chopped
- 2 tablespoons Chopped fresh cilantro freshly ground black pepper
- ⅓ cup White or gold tequila
- ¾ cup Fresh lime juice
- 3 large Cloves garlic, crushed
- 3 mediums Tomatoes, diced
- 1 tablespoon Minced jalapeno pinch of sugar

Directions:

a) Place fish in a non-aluminium dish large enough to hold it in a single layer. Combine tequila, triple sec, lime juice, salt, garlic and 2 teaspoons oil and pour over fish, rubbing all over. Cover and marinate for $\frac{1}{2}$ hour at room temperature or up to 3 hours in the refrigerator, turning occasionally.

b) Just before serving, combine tomatoes, onions, chilies, cilantro, sugar and salt to taste. Heat the grill to very hot. remove fish from marinade, pat dry (reserving marinade) and brush lightly with 1 teaspoons oil and grind pepper over the surface. Cook on a greased grill for about 4 minutes per side or until flesh is opaque.

c) Meanwhile, boil marinade in saucepan for 2 minutes, remove and discard garlic cloves, and spoon a little of it over the fish, Spoon the tomato salsa alongside and serve.

6. Margarita beef with orange salsa

Yield: 5 Servings

Ingredient

- ⅔ cup Frozen Orange Juice concentrate, thawed
- ½ cup Tequila
- ⅓ cup Fresh lime juice
- 2 tablespoons Olive oil
- 2 tablespoons Chopped fresh ginger
- 2 Med. cloves garlic, crushed
- 1 teaspoon Salt
- 1 teaspoon Dried oregano leaves
- ¼ teaspoon Ground red pepper
- 1½ pounds Well-trimmed boneless beef
- 1 Round steak, 1 inch thick
- 1 Orange salsa (rec. follows)

Directions:

a) Combine orange juice concentrate, Tequila, lime juice, oil, ginger, garlic, salt, oregano and red pepper. Place steak in a plastic bag: add marinade, turning to coat. Close bag securely and marinate, refrigerated, for 4 hours, or up to overnight.

b) Prepare orange salsa Remove steak from marinade; discard marinade. Place steak on grill over medium coals.

c) Grill 22 to 26 minutes for medium-rare to medium doneness, turning once. Remove steak to carving board; let stand 10 minutes. Carve steak crosswise into thin slices: Arrange on serving platter. Garnish with cilantro and lime; serve with orange salsa. Makes 5 to 6 servings.

7. Margarita shrimp with fettuccine

Yield: 2 Servings

Ingredient

- 12 large Shrimp -- peeled and
- Deveined
- ½ cup Tequila
- 3 tablespoons Fresh lemon juice
- 2 Eggs
- 2 tablespoons Water
- ¼ cup Olive oil
- All-purpose flour
- ½ cup Unsalted butter
- 3 Thin lemon slices
- 4 Green onions -- chopped
- 2 teaspoons Minced ginger -- peeled
- 2 teaspoons Minced garlic
- 1 teaspoon All-purpose flour

- 1 cup Dry white wine

- 6 ounces Fettuccine

- Chopped fresh dill

- 2 hours. Drain shrimp.

Directions:

a) Mix shrimp, tequila and lemon juice in medium bowl. Cover and refrigerate Whisk eggs and water in medium bowl.

b) Season with salt and pepper. Heat oil in large skillet over medium heat. Dip shrimp into egg mixture, then into flour; shake off excess. Place shrimp in skillet and sauté until pink and cooked through, about 2 minutes per side. Transfer shrimp to plate lined with paper towels and drain. Discard oil.

c) In same skillet, melt $\frac{1}{4}$ c butter over medium heat. Add lemon and green onions and sauté 3 minutes. Add ginger and garlic and sauté 2 minutes.

d) Stir in flour. Gradually mix in wine; boil until reduced to glaze, about 2 minutes. Add remaining butter and whisk until melted. Discard lemon. Return shrimp to skillet and heat through.

e) Meanwhile cook pasta in salted water. Drain. Divide pasta between plates.

f) Top with shrimp. Pour sauce over. Sprinkle with dill and serve.

8. Margarita steaks

Yield: 2 Servings

Ingredient

- ¼ cup Tequila
- 2 tablespoons Sugar
- 1 tablespoon Cilantro; chopped, fresh
- 1 teaspoon Lime peel
- ½ teaspoon Salt
- 2 tablespoons Lime juice
- 1 Jalapeno; seeded, chopped
- 2 T-bone steak

Directions:

a) In rectangular glass baking dish, combine all Ingredients except steaks; mix well. Place steaks in mixture, turning to coat both sides. Cover; refrigerate at least 4 hours to marinate, turning steaks once. Heat grill.

b) When ready to grill, remove steaks from marinade; reserve marinade. Place steaks on gas grill over medium heat or on charcoal grill 4 - - 6 inches from medium coals; cover grill. Cook 10 - 15 minutes or until steaks are of desired doneness, turning once and brushing occasionally with marinade

9. Margarita's pasta primavera

Yield: 4 Servings

Ingredient

- 1 cup Low-fat cottage cheese
- 1 tablespoon Fresh lemon juice
- 8 ounces Thin spaghetti
- 1 tablespoon Acceptable vegetable oil
- 1/4 cup Chopped scallions
- 1/2 cup Chopped onions
- 1 Clove garlic, minced
- 1/4 teaspoon Freshly ground black pepper,
- Or to taste
- 2 cups Sliced fresh mushrooms
- 1 cup Sliced green bell pepper
- 1 1/2 cup Sliced carrots
- 10 ounces Frozen no-salt-added
- Broccoli, steamed

Directions:

a) Drain any liquid off of cottage cheese. In a bowl, combine cottage cheese and lemon juice. Set aside.

b) Prepare spaghetti according to package Directions, omitting salt.

c) Drain thoroughly.

d) Meanwhile, heat oil in skillet over medium-high heat. Add scallions, onions, garlic, and black pepper and sauté 1 minute4. Add mushrooms and stir 1 minute. Then add bell pepper, carrots, and broccoli and stir for another 3-4 minutes. Set aside.

e) In another bowl, toss spaghetti and cottage cheese mixture to coat evenly. Top with sautéed vegetables.

10. Shark margarita

Yield: 8 Servings

Ingredient

- 8 Shark steaks; 1-inch thick
- ⅓ cup Lime juice
- 1 teaspoon Lime rind; grated
- 2 Cloves garlic; minced
- ¼ teaspoon Ground ginger
- ½ cup Vegetable oil
- 1 teaspoon Pepper; freshly ground
- 1 tablespoon Liquid honey; or maple syrup

Directions:

a) Rinse shark in cold water and pat dry. In a large bowl, combine lime juice and rind, garlic, ginger, vegetable oil, pepper and honey.

b) Add shark, stirring to coat well. Cover with plastic wrap and marinate at room temperature for 30 minutes or refrigerate for up to 1 hour, turning shark occasionally.

c) Drain shark, reserving marinade. Grill shark steaks 4-inches from medium-hot coals on a barbecue, or broil in oven on a medium-high setting, brushing with reserved marinade, for 5 to 6 minutes per side.

11. Beef and tequila stew

Yield: 6 servings

Ingredient

- 2 pounds Meat
- ¼ cup Unbleached Flour
- ¼ cup Vegetable Oil
- ½ cup Onion; Chopped, 1 Medium
- 2 each Bacon; Slices, Cut Up
- ¼ cup Carrot; Chopped
- ¼ cup Celery; Chopped
- ¼ cup Tequila
- ¾ cup Tomato Juice
- 2 tablespoons Cilantro; Fresh, Snipped
- 1½ teaspoon Salt
- 15 ounces Garbanzo Beans; 1 Can
- 4 cups Tomatoes; Chopped, 4 Medium

- 2 each Cloves Garlic; Finely Chopped

Directions:

a) Coat beef with flour. Heat oil in 10-inch skillet until hot. Cook and stir beef in oil over medium heat until brown.

b) Remove beef with slotted spoon and drain. Cook and stir onion and bacon in same skillet until bacon is crisp. Stir in beef and remaining Ingredients. heat to boiling; reduce heat.

c) Cover and simmer until beef is tender, about 1 hour.

12. Broiled chicken with tequila and lime

Yield: 4 Servings

Ingredient

- 4 Chicken breast halves; skin bone
- ⅓ cup Tequila
- 2 tablespoons Honey
- 1 Lime; zest and juice
- ½ teaspoon Ground cumin

Directions:

a) Preheat the broiler. Pound the breasts lightly to flatten evenly. In a medium bowl, combine the tequila, honey, zest and juice and ground cumin.

b) Stir to mix well. Add the chicken and turn several times until the chicken is well-coated with the marinade. Place the chicken breasts on a broiler pan. Broil about 4" from the heat, turning once and basting several times with the sauce for the first 4 minutes, until the chicken is

browned outside and white to the center,
6 to 8 minutes' total.

13. Honey-lime-tequila chicken

Yield: 8 servings

Ingredient

- 4 Skinless boneless chicken breast halves
- 2 tablespoons Honey
- ⅔ cup Fresh lime juice
- ¼ cup Tequila
- 2 Cloves garlic; minced
- 1 Yellow onion; minced
- 1 Red pepper; minced

Directions:

a) Combine marinade Ingredients and pour over the chicken breasts. Marinate for at least 1 hour.

b) Drain the marinade and grill on each side about 7-8 minutes per side or until no pink remains.

14. Pan-seared salmon

Yield: 4 servings

Ingredient

- 4 Italian plum tomatoes about 8 oz.
- 1 Serrano or jalapeno chile coarsely chopped
- ¼ Red onion coarsely chopped
- 4 Salmon fillets bones and skin removed
- 1 Garlic clove
- ⅓ cup Tequila
- ½ teaspoon Salt
- ¼ teaspoon Cracked black pepper
- 1 tablespoon Balsamic vinegar
- 1 tablespoon Olive oil
- 3 tablespoons mild red chili powder
- 6 tablespoons Olive oil

Directions:

a) Prepare the Tomato-Tequila Vinaigrette and set aside.

b) Rub the salmon fillets with the chile powder. Heat the olive oil in a frying pan over medium-high heat, add the fillets without crowding and sear 3 to 4 minutes per side, depending on the desired degree of doneness.

c) To serve, place the salmon fillets on four plates, stir the vinaigrette and pour it over the fillets.

d) Blackened Tomato-Tequila Vinaigrette: To blacken the tomatoes, preheat a heavy skillet over high heat. Add the whole tomatoes and cook, turning occasionally, until the tomato skins split and are blackened, about 5 minutes. Remove and let cool. Peel the tomatoes, discard the stem ends and coarsely chop the tomatoes.

e) Combine the tomatoes, chile, onion, garlic, tequila, salt and pepper in a nonreactive saucepan and simmer over medium-high heat for 10 minutes, stirring occasionally. Pour the contents into a blender or food processor and blend 1 minute.

f) Strain through a fine-mesh sieve into a bowl. Add the vinegar and olive oil and mix well. Taste for seasoning.

15.   Pasta with tequila, avocado and shrimp

Yield: 4 servings

Ingredient

- 8 large Tomatoes; cored and seeded
- 2 teaspoons Coarse salt
- $\frac{1}{2}$ teaspoon Freshly-ground black pepper
- 1 pounds Fettuccine
- 1 pounds Medium shrimp; peeled and deveined
- 1 teaspoon Crushed red pepper flakes
- 8 tablespoons Unsalted butter
- $\frac{1}{2}$ cup Tequila
- 1 Avocado; seed removed, peeled and diced
- 1 bunch Cilantro; chopped

Directions:

a) Puree tomatoes in a blender until smooth, adding a tablespoon or 2 of water if dry.

Reserve. Fill a large stockpot with water and bring to a rolling boil. Add salt and pasta and cook until al dente, about 8 minutes. Drain in a colander. Melt 4 tablespoons of butter in a large skillet over high heat.

b) Sauté shrimp with salt, pepper and red pepper flakes until pink orange, about 1 minute per side. Add tequila and flambé. With a slotted spoon, transfer shrimp to a platter, leaving butter in pan.

c) Add reserved tomato puree, bring to a boil and cook until reduced by about one third. Adjust seasonings to taste. Break apart remaining butter into small pieces and stir into sauce along with shrimp.

d) Once smooth, remove from heat, and ladle over bowls of warm fettuccine. Garnish with avocado and chopped cilantro.

16. Yellowtail snapper with mango

Yield: 4 Servings

Ingredient

- 4 Snapper Fillets (6 Ounces Each); Skinned
- 1 cup Cornmeal
- 2 tablespoons Extra-Virgin Olive Oil; Divided
- 2 Shallots; Chopped Fine
- 3 tablespoons Tarragon Wine Vinegar
- ¼ cup Tequila
- 1 cup Chicken Stock
- ¼ cup Orange Juice Concentrate
- 1½ cup Mangoes; Diced
- 2 tablespoons Fresh Chives; Chopped
- Salt and Freshly Ground Pepper to Taste

Directions:

a) Heat oven to 375 degrees. Dip each fish fillet in the cornmeal and dust off excess.

b) In an oven-proof sauté pan large enough to hold the fillets without crowding, heat 1 tablespoon of the olive oil. Add the snapper and sauté for 1 minute. Turn fillet over; then transfer the pan to the oven, and bake the fish for 4 to 5 minutes. the fish should then be opaque, not translucent.

c) While the fish is baking, in a medium saucepan, heat 1 tablespoon olive oil. Sweat the shallots and when translucent, add the vinegar. Let reduce until almost dry. Add the tequila and let reduce by half. Stir in the stock, orange juice concentrate and mangoes. Let simmer for 5 minutes.

d) Pour into blender and process until very smooth. Add the chives and adjust the seasoning.

e) Spoon about 2 tablespoons of sauce onto each dinner plate and set the cooked fish in the center.

f) For a beautiful presentation, decorate with diced mango, or with purple basil and chives.

17.   Tequila-orange chicken

Yield: 6 servings

Ingredient

- ½ cup Orange Juice
- ¼ cup Tequila
- 2 tablespoons Vlasic hot jalapeno peppers
- ½ teaspoon Grated orange peel
- 1 can (10-1/2oz.) chicken gravy
- 3 each Whole chicken breasts

Directions:

a) To make sauce: In 1-quart saucepan, combine juice, tequila, peppers and peel. Over high heat, heat to boiling. Reduce heat to low.

b) Simmer, uncovered 10 minutes or until mixture is reduced by half.

c) Add gravy, heat through, stirring constantly.

d) On grill rack, place chicken, skin side up, directly above medium coals. Grill uncovered 1 hour or until tender and juices run clear, turning and brushing with sauce during the last 30 minutes.

e) To broil: Arrange chicken, skin side up, on rack in broiler pan.

f) Broil 6 inches from heat 40 minutes or until tender and juices run clear, turning and brushing often with sauce during the last 20 minutes.

18.   Tequila-lime shrimp

Yield: 1 Servings

Ingredient

- ½ Stick margarine
- 2 tablespoons Olive oil
- 2 Garlic cloves, minced
- 1½ pounds Medium shrimp, shelled and deveined
- 3 tablespoons Tequila
- 1½ tablespoon Lime juice
- ½ teaspoon Salt
- ½ teaspoon Chili powder
- 4 tablespoons Coarsely chopped fresh cilantro

Directions:

a) Pat shrimp dry with paper towels. Heat margarine and oil in a large skillet over a medium heat. Add garlic and shrimp;

cook about 2 minutes, stirring occasionally.

b) Stir in tequila, lime juice, salt, and chili powder. Cook 2 minutes more or until most of the liquid is evaporated and shrimp is pink and glazed. Add cilantro.

c) Serve over hot, cooked rice, garnished with lime wedges.

19.   Tequila pasta Quattro fromaggio

Yield: 4 Servings

Ingredient

- 1 tablespoon Stick margarine or butter
- 1 tablespoon All-purpose flour
- $\frac{1}{2}$ teaspoon Pepper
- $\frac{1}{4}$ teaspoon Salt
- 1 can Evaporated skim milk (12-oz.)
- $\frac{1}{4}$ cup Shredded fontina cheese (1 oz.)
- $\frac{1}{4}$ cup Crumbled gorgonzola or other blue cheese -- (1 oz.
- $\frac{1}{4}$ cup Diced camembert cheese; (1 oz.)
- 6 cups Hot cooked rigatoni; (9 oz. uncooked)
- 2 tablespoons Chopped fresh basil
- $\frac{1}{4}$ cup Finely grated fresh parmesan cheese -- (1 oz.)

Directions:

a) Melt margarine in a large saucepan over medium heat. Add flour; cook 30 seconds, stirring constantly with whisk. Add pepper, salt, and milk, and bring to a simmer, stirring frequently.

b) Remove from heat, and add fontina, Gorgonzola, and Camembert cheeses, stirring until cheeses melt. Stir in pasta and basil; spoon into each of 4 bowls. Sprinkle with Parmesan cheese.

20. Sweet corn, jicama salad with tequila

Yield: 4 servings

Ingredient

- 6 Ears of corn
- 2 Jicama
- 1 Red pepper, finely diced
- 1 Yellow pepper, finely diced
- 3 Baby spinach
- 2 tablespoons Pine nuts
- Dressing:
- Juice of 3 limes
- 2 tablespoons Tequila
- 1 teaspoon White wine vinegar
- ½ cup Olive oil
- 1 pinch Cumin
- 1 pinch Cayenne

Directions:

a) Cook corn in salted water until tender. Remove corn from cob. Peel and julienne jicama. Dice red and yellow peppers.

b) Put all Ingredients for dressing in a medium sauce pot except oil and bring to a boil. Slowly emulsify oil into base and reserve.

c) Toss spinach, jicama and corn together and dress. Divide evenly between six plates and garnish with peppers and pinon.

21. Pork tenderloin in tequila

Yield: 6 Servings

Ingredient

- 2 pounds Pork Tenderloin
- ¼ cup Vegetable Oil
- 2 Cloves Garlic
- ¼ cup Carrot; Chopped
- ¼ cup Celery; Chopped
- ¼ cup Lime Juice
- ¼ cup Tequila
- 1 tablespoon Red Chiles; Ground
- 1 teaspoon Salt
- 1 teaspoon Oregano Leaves; Dried
- 1 teaspoon Thyme Leaves; Dried
- ¼ teaspoon Pepper
- 4 cups Tomatoes; Chopped
- ¼ cup Onion; Chopped

- 1 Bay Leaf
- ¼ cup Parsley; Snipped

Directions:

a) Spread mustard over the pork tenderloin. Heat oil and garlic in a 10" skillet until hot. Cook pork in oil over medium heat until brown.

b) Remove garlic. Stir in remaining Ingredients except the parsley. Heat to boiling then reduce the heat. Cover and simmer until pork is done, about 30 minutes. Remove the bay leaf and sprinkle with the parsley.

c) Serve.

22. Chickens marinated in margarita

Yield: 4 Servings

Ingredient

- 4 Poussins (baby chickens) OR Cornish game hens
- ½ cup Fresh lime juice
- ⅓ cup Golden tequila
- ¼ cup Olive oil
- 2 tablespoons Cointreau
- 2 Garlic cloves; peel/mince
- Salt and pepper

Directions:

a) Remove backbones from chickens. Flatten chickens with palm of hand.

b) In large bowl, combine lime juice, tequila, olive oil, Cointreau and garlic. Add chickens and turn to coat. Cover and marinate, turning once or twice, up to 2 hours at room temperature or overnight in refrigerator.

c) Return to room temperature before cooking.

d) Remove chickens from marinade and arrange, skin-side up, in shallow baking pan. Season with salt and pepper to taste.

e) Bake at 400 degrees on upper rack of oven, basting occasionally with marinade, until skin is golden and juices from thighs, pierced at their thickest part, run pinkish-yellow, 25 to 30 minutes.

23. Santa fe shrimp with tequila sauce

Yield: 1 Servings

Ingredient

- 3 Green New Mexico chiles, roasted, peeled, stems and seeds removed, chopped
- 24 large Shrimp, shells removed, butterflied
- 2 tablespoons Butter
- 2 tablespoons Tequila juice from 3 limes
- ½ cup Whipping cream
- 1 tablespoon Grated lime peel

Directions:

a) These spicy shrimp can be served as an appetizer or an entree. A dry white wine can be substituted for the tequila if you prefer.

b) Sauté the shrimp and green chile in the butter until they start to lose their translucency. Remove the shrimp and keep warm. Increase the heat and add the tequila and lime juice.

c) While stirring, add the cream and zest and continue to stir until the sauce thickens. Return the shrimp to the pan and heat for 2-3 minutes or until the shrimp are done. Serves 4-6.

24. Sweet potato and Tequila soup

Yield: 4 Servings

Ingredient

- 3 medium Sweet potatoes
- 4 tablespoons Tequila
- ¼ cup Unsalted butter; room temp.
- Fresh grated nutmeg to taste
- ½ teaspoon Salt (or to taste)
- Fresh ground white pepper to taste

Directions:

a) Scrub unpeeled sweet potatoes, cut in large chunks and cook in lightly salted boiling water until tender. Then pour off water, cover pan and let potatoes 'fluff' about 5 minutes.

b) Quickly peel potatoes, add 2 tablespoons tequila, butter and nutmeg. Beat with an electric mixer or process in a food processor until smooth.

c) Taste and add salt, white pepper and 2 more tablespoons tequila, if desired. Serve warm. Makes 4 to 6 servings.

MARGARITA DESSERTS

25.   Margarita pie

Yield: 10 Servings

Ingredient

- 1 pack Frozen strawberries in syrup thawed (10 ounces)
- 1 pack Cream cheese, softened (8 oz.
- ½ cup Thawed Margarita mix
- 4 ounces Cool whip - thawed
- 1 pack graham cracker pie crust

Directions:

a) Place strawberries, cream cheese and margarita mix concentrate in blender or food processor.

b) Cover and blend on medium speed until well blended. Pour mixture into medium bowl; fold in whipped topping.

c) Pour into pie crust. Freeze 4 to 6 hours or until firm. Let stand at room temperature 5 to 10 minutes before cutting.

26. Frozen strawberry margarita dessert

Yield: 8 Servings

Ingredient

- 1¼ cup Finely crushed pretzels
- ¼ cup Sugar
- ½ cup Butter or margarine; melted
- 1 can Sweetened condensed milk; 14 oz.
- ¼ cup Lime juice
- 2 tablespoons Tequila
- 2 tablespoons Orange liqueur
- 1 pack Strawberries in syrup; 10 oz. thawed
- 1 cup Whipping cream

Directions:

a) To make crust: Combine pretzels, sugar and melted butter. Press firmly into bottom of 8" spring form pan. Chill.

b) For filling, combine condensed milk, lime juice, tequila and orange liqueur. Beat until smooth. Add strawberries, beat at low speed until well-blended.

c) Fold in whipping cream. Pour over crust, freeze 4 - 6 hours or until firm.

d) Let stand at room temperature 15 minutes before serving.

27. Frozen strawberry margarita pie

Yield: 1 Servings

Ingredient

- 1¼ Finely crushed pretzels
- ¼ Lime juice
- ¼ Sugar
- 4 Tequila
- ½ + 2 T. melted butter or m
- 2 Triple sec or other orange
- 14 Can sweetened condensed Milk
- 1 Red Food Coloring
- 1 Chopped fresh
- 1 Whipping cream -- whipped

Directions:

a) Combine pretzel crumbs, sugar, and margarine; press firmly on bottom and up sides to rim of lightly buttered 9" pie plate.

b) In bowl, combine sweetened condensed milk, chopped strawberries, lime juice, tequila, triple sec and food coloring, if desired. Mix well. Fold in whipped cream. Pour into prepared crust.

c) Freeze 4 hours or until firm. Let stand 10 minutes before serving. Garnish as desired. >> Freeze leftovers. -- Makes one 9" pie MARGARITA PIE: Omit strawberries and red food coloring.

d) Increase lime juice to ⅓ c. and add green food coloring if desired. Proceed as above. Freeze 4 hours. Garnish as desired. Freeze leftovers.

28. Mango key lime margaritas

Yield: 2 Servings

Ingredient

- 2 Tequila
- 1 Cointreau
- ¼ Fresh mango; peeled and chopped
- ½ cup Fresh orange juice
- ½ Key or Mexican lime; juice only
- 1 cup Ice; crushed
- 2 slices Key or Mexican lime (garnish)

Directions:

a) Combine tequila, Cointreau, mango, orange juice, lime juice and ice in a blender and blend until slushy.

b) Garnish with lime slices.

29.   Margarita cheesecake

Yield: 12 servings

Ingredient

- 1¼ cup Vanilla wafer cookie crumbs
- ¼ cup Unsalted butter, melted
- 3 8ounce packages cream cheese
- Room temperature
- 2 cups Sour cream
- 1¼ cup Sugar
- 3 tablespoons Grand Marnier
- 3 tablespoons Gold tequila
- 3 tablespoons Juice, lime
- 2 teaspoons Grated lime peel
- 4 large Eggs

Directions:

a) Preheat oven to 350 degrees. Mix cookie crumbs and butter in medium bowl until blended.

b) Press mixture onto bottom and 1-inch up sides of 9inchdiameter spring form pan with 2 3/4inch high sides. Refrigerate while preparing filling.

c) Using electric mixer, beat cream cheese in large bowl until fluffy.

d) Add 1 cup sour cream, 1 cup sugar, Grand Marnier, tequila, lime juice and lime peel and beat until well blended. Add eggs 1 at a time, beating just until blended after each addition.

e) Pour filling into crust. Bake until center is softly set, about 50 minutes. Maintain oven temperature. Mix remaining 1 cup sour cream, $\frac{1}{4}$ cup sugar and 1 tablespoon lime juice in small bowl. Pour over cheesecake. Using spatula, smooth top. Bake cheesecake 5 minutes longer.

f) Transfer pan to rack and cool completely. Refrigerate until well chilled, at least 4 hours or overnight.

g) Run knife around pan sides to loosen cake. Remove pan sides. Garnish cake with lime slices.

30. Margarita pot de crème

Yield: 8 Servings

Ingredient

- ⅔ cup Granulated sugar
- 2 teaspoons Cornstarch
- 1 tablespoon Finely grated lime rind
- ⅓ cup Lime juice
- 2 tablespoons Each tequila and Triple Sec
- 4 Egg yolks
- 1 cup Whipping cream
- 2 cups Sliced strawberries
- 8 Strips lime rind

Directions:

a) In heavy saucepan over medium heat, whisk sugar with cornstarch. Whisk in rind and juice, tequila, Triple Sec and egg yolks; cook, stirring, for 4 minutes or until thickened and bubbles break on surface.

b) Transfer to bowl; place plastic wrap on surface. Refrigerate for 1 hour or until very cold.

31. Strawberry margarita mousse

Yield: 5 Servings

Ingredient

- 4 cups Whole strawberries, hulled
- 1 cup Sugar
- 3 tablespoons Boiling water
- 4 teaspoons Unflavored gelatin
- $\frac{1}{4}$ cup Tequila
- 1 tablespoon Triple sec or other orange-flavored liqueur
- 2 cups Plain nonfat yogurt

Directions:

a) Place strawberries in a blender, and process until smooth. Pour into a large bowl; stir in sugar. Cover and let stand 30 minutes, stirring occasionally.

b) Combine boiling water and gelatin in a small bowl; let stand 5 minutes or until gelatin dissolves, stirring constantly.

Add the tequila and triple sec, and stir well. Stir the gelatin mixture into the strawberry mixture.

c) Cover and chill for 10 minutes or until the mixture begins to thicken. Add yogurt (at room temperature), stirring with a wire whisk until well-blended.

d) Divide the mixture evenly among 5 margarita glasses or large stemmed glasses; cover and chill at least 4 hours or until set.

32.   Margarita fruit salad

Yield: 1 Serving

Ingredient

- 1 Cantaloupe and honeydew melon, cut in chunks
- 2 Oranges and grapefruit, peeled and sectioned
- 1 Mango, peeled and diced
- 2 cups Strawberries, halved
- ½ cup Sugar
- ⅓ cup Orange juice
- 3 tablespoons Tequila
- 3 tablespoons Orange liqueur
- 3 tablespoons Lime juice
- 1 cup Coarsely grated fresh coconut

Directions:

a) Combine fruit, set aside. In small saucepan, cook sugar and orange juice over medium-high heat, stirring, for 3 minutes or until sugar dissolves.

b) Stir in tequila, liqueur, and lime juice. Let cool to room temperature.

c) Combine with fruit. Cover and refrigerate for at least two hours or overnight. Just before serving sprinkle with coconut.

33. Spanish almond cake laced with tequila

Yield: 8 servings

Ingredient
- 1 cup + 2 Tablespoons almonds; lightly roasted
- 1 cup Flour; all-purpose
- 1¼ teaspoon Baking powder
- ¼ teaspoon Salt
- ½ pounds Butter; unsalted
- 1 cup Sugar
- Freshly grated nutmeg
- ½ pint Heavy cream
- 3 tablespoons Powdered sugar
- 4 Eggs
- ¼ teaspoon Pure almond extract
- 3 tablespoons Tequila anejo
- 2 teaspoons Orange zest
- 1 teaspoon Lemon zest
- ¼ teaspoon Nutmeg; grated
- Sliced mangoes
- ¼ teaspoon Vanilla extract
- 1 tablespoon Tequila anejo

Directions:

a) Finely grind all almonds. Set 2 tablespoons ground nuts aside. Mix remaining nuts with flour, baking powder and salt and set aside.

b) Cream butter and sugar with an electric mixer. Add eggs, one at a time, mixing well, blend in the almond extract, tequila, citrus zests and $\frac{1}{4}$ teaspoon grated nutmeg. Mix in almond/flour mixture until incorporated. Spread batter into a $9\frac{1}{2}$-inch-by-2-inch pan (or a spring form pan) that has been buttered and dusted with flour.

c) Sprinkle with remaining ground almonds. Place in preheated 325-degree oven on the middle rack and bake until tester comes out clean (about 40-45 minutes). Cool 10 minutes; remove from pan by inverting on a platter. Sprinkle with confectioners' sugar and freshly grated nutmeg; garnish. Serve with a tasty coffee drink or eggnog.

d) Nutritional analysis per serving: 420 calories, 28 grams fat, 34 grams carbohydrates, 135 milligrams cholesterol, 189 milligrams sodium, 61 percent of calories from fat.

e) Mexican whipped cream: In chilled stainless-steel mixing bowl with chilled beaters, whip cream until it thickens slightly. Slowly add powdered sugar, vanilla and tequila and beat until it forms stiff mounds.

34. Strawberries bowl with tequila

Yield: 6 Servings

Ingredient
- 6 cups Halved strawberries
- ½ cup Orange juice
- ¼ cup Tequila
- 2 teaspoons Freshly ground pepper
- 2 teaspoons Balsamic vinegar
- Mint sprigs, (optional)

Directions:

a) Combine the Ingredients in a bowl, and toss well.
b) Cover and chill 3 hours, stirring occasionally.

35. Lentil cakes with nopalito cactus salsa

Yield: 1 servings

Ingredient
- 1 cup Red lentils
- 1 cup Green French lentils
- 1 cup Mixed peppers; sweet and hot,
- ¼ cup Scallions; sliced
- ¼ cup Onions; diced
- 2 Eggs
- 1 cup Whole wheat flour
- ¼ cup Snipped chives
- ¼ cup Carrots and celery; diced very small
- Salt and pepper
- 1 Nopalito cactus; diced small
- ½ cup Mixed peppers
- ½ cup Mixed citrus supremes. chopped
- ½ cup Diced tomatoes
- 1 tablespoon Chives; sliced
- 3 tablespoons Cilantro; chopped
- 2 tablespoons Onion; diced
- 2 Limes; Juice of
- 2 tablespoons Olive oil
- Salt and pepper
- ½ cup Tequila

Directions:

a) Cook lentils separately in salted water until tender, about 15 minutes for the red and 25 minutes for the green. Drain and pat dry.
b) Puree red lentils and mix with whole green lentils and remaining Ingredients. Divide into 24 equal portions and pan fry until golden brown.
c) Salsa: Mix all Ingredients together.

36. Tequila spiked watermelon soup

Yield: 1 servings

Ingredient

- 1 cup Sugar
- ½ cup Tequila
- ¾ cup Water
- ¼ cup Triple sec
- 1 cup Heavy cream
- 2 tablespoons Watermelon juice
- 2 tablespoons Triple sec
- 3 cups Watermelon; seeded and diced
- 2½ cup Melon puree
- 1½ cup Tequila syrup
- ¼ cup Tequila
- ¼ cup Melon juice
- 2 Limes; juiced
- 4 tablespoons Melon

- 1 tablespoon Triple sec
- 1 Lime blanched in tequila syrup; Zest of

Directions:

a) Make tequila syrup: Combine all syrup Ingredients. Place on medium heat until sugar dissolves. Chill until cold.

b) Make triple sec whipped cream garnish: Combine whipped cream Ingredients and beat to stiff peaks. Pipe rosettes on waxed paper-lined pan. Freeze.

c) Make soup: In a food processor place 3 cups of watermelon. Pour out excess juice and reserve.

d) Puree watermelon until smooth. In a bowl combine the melon puree, the reserved juice, $1\frac{1}{2}$ cups tequila syrup, $\frac{1}{4}$ cup tequila, juice of two limes and chill. In another small bowl combine 4 tablespoons diced melons for garnish, 1 tablespoon triple sec, and lime zest and chill.

e) To serve, place whipped cream garnish in the bottom of a Kosher salt-rimmed bowl or glass. Pour 6 ounces of soup into the bowl or glass. Garnish with 1 tablespoon of the diced melons and sprinkle with salt.

37. Corn crab cakes with margarita butter

Yield: 1 Servings

Ingredient

- 2 pounds Crab meat; cleaned
- 2 tablespoons Mustard
- 2 teaspoons Worcestershire sauce
- ½ teaspoon Cayenne pepper
- 1 cup Breadcrumbs
- 1 cup Mayonnaise
- 2 Serrano pepper; seeded and diced
- ½ cup Roasted corn
- ½ Red bell pepper; diced
- ½ Red onion; diced
- 2 tablespoons Fresh cilantro; minced
- Salt and pepper
- 1 cup Chicken stock
- ½ cup Tequila

- ¼ cup Lime juice
- 1 cup White wine
- ¼ cup Heavy cream
- 2 pounds Unsalted butter
- Salt and white pepper

Directions:

a) CRAB CAKES Roast corn in oven. Combine all Ingredients except mayonnaise, mustard and crabmeat and mix well. Add crabmeat and toss with mustard and mayonnaise. Form into cakes and brown in skillet.

b) TEQUILA LIME BUTTER Combine all liquids in large pot and reduce to one-quarter of the volume. Cut butter into one-inch squares, and add two cubes at a time to liquid, continually whisking. In blender, pulse three to five times until emulsified. Salt and pepper to taste.

MARGARITA CONDIMENTS

38. Grapefruit margarita sauce

Yield: 4 Servings

Ingredient

- 4 shallots
- 2 jalapenos
- 1 Tablespoon vegetable oil
- 1 bunch cilantro stems
- 2 cups grapefruit juice
- ½ cups chicken stock
- 3 oz. tequila
- ¼ c lime juice
- 2 Tablespoon corn starch, dissolved in 2¼ c each grapefruit, orange and lime segments,
- 2 Tablespoon chopped cilantro
- 1 oz. Cointreau
- Salt

Directions:

a) Heat oil in a medium saucepan over medium-high heat. Add shallots, jalapenos, cilantro stems and sweat for 3 minutes. Add grapefruit juice, chicken stock, tequila and lime juice. Bring to a boil.

b) Stirring constantly, gradually pour in cornstarch mixture just until sauce begins to thicken -- you will not need to use it all. Simmer about 20 minutes. Strain through a fine sieve. Fold in citrus segments, cilantro and Cointreau. Season to taste with salt.

39. Monterey jack tequila fondue

Yield: 6 servings

Ingredient

- 10 ounces Chicken broth
- ⅓ cup Tequila
- 1 pounds Monterey Jack cheese, grated
- 1½ tablespoon Cornstarch

Directions:

a) Bring the broth and tequila to boil. Reduce heat and add the grated cheese, stirring until smooth. Stir in cornstarch and continue to cook until thick and bubbly.

b) Pour into fondue pot and set over low heat. Serve with vegetables dippers and salsa. Makes 6 servings.

40. Margarita glaze for poultry

Yield: 1 Servings

Ingredient

- ¼ cup Honey
- ¼ cup Triple sec
- ¼ cup Lime juice
- ¼ cup Tequila

Directions:

a) Mix

41. Margarita jalapeno salsa

Yield: 1 Servings

Ingredient

- ½ cup Cubed tomato (1/2-inch cubes)
- ½ cup Medium-fine-chopped red or white onion
- 4 Or more fresh Jalapeno chiles; very finely minced
- 1 Clove garlic; minced
- ½ teaspoon Salt; or to taste
- ¼ cup Gold or white tequila

Directions:

a) Combine all Ingredients and let stand at least 30 minutes at room temperature.

b) Taste and adjust seasonings.

c) Makes about 1-½ cups.

42. Margarita marinade

Yield: 1 batch

Ingredient

- 10 ounces Can diced tomatoes
- And green chilies, drained
- ¼ cup Orange juice
- ¼ cup Tequila
- ¼ cup Vegetable oil
- 2 tablespoons Fresh lime juice
- 1 tablespoon Honey
- 1 teaspoon Minced fresh garlic
- 1 teaspoon Grated lime peel

Directions:

a) In large plastic food bag, combine all Ingredients except meat.

b) Mix well.

43.   Margarita brine

Yield: 1 batch

Ingredient

- 10 ounces Can diced tomatoes
- And green chilies, drained
- ¼ cup Orange juice
- ¼ cup Tequila
- ¼ cup Vegetable oil
- 2 pounds Pork tenderloin, or
- Chicken breasts, or
- 2 tablespoons Fresh lime juice
- 1 tablespoon Honey
- 1 teaspoon Minced fresh garlic
- 1 teaspoon Grated lime peel

Directions:

a) In large plastic food bag, mix all Ingredients.

44. Margarita shrimp marinade

Yield: 1 servings

Ingredient

- ¼ cup Vegetable oil
- 3 tablespoons Fresh lime juice
- 3 tablespoons Tequila
- 2 tablespoons Triple sec
- 1 large Jalapeno chili; seeded, minced
- 1½ teaspoon Grated lime peel
- 1 teaspoon Chili powder
- 1 teaspoon Sugar
- ½ teaspoon Coarse salt

Directions:

a) Mix all Ingredients in small bowl. Let stand 15 minutes.

b) Cover and refrigerate.

45.   Tequila lime relish

Yield: 4 servings

Ingredient

- 2 Limes, peeled and cut into
- Sections
- 2 ounces Tequila, preferably Cuervo
- Gold
- 1 small White onion, diced
- 2 tablespoons Hot pepper jelly
- 2 tablespoons White wine
- 1 tablespoon Sherry or Champagne vinegar
- 1 tablespoon Fresh cilantro, chopped
- 1 teaspoon Toasted cumin seeds

Directions:

a) Mix all the Ingredients and let stand for 1 hour.

b) For garnish, use carrot peels and chives.

MARGARITA APPETIZERS

46.   Margarita balls

Yield: 1 Servings

Ingredient

- 1 pack (12-ounce) vanilla wafers
- ½ cup Pretzel crumbs; (about 1 cup pretzels)
- 1 pack (16-ounce) confectioners' sugar; sifted
- ¾ cup Frozen margarita or limeade concentrate; thawed
- 2 packs (3-ounce) cream cheese
- 1 teaspoon Tequila; or to taste, optional
- 1 teaspoon Triple Sec; (orange liqueur), or to taste, optional
- Rind from 1 lime; grated fine, (divided use)
- 1 Shaker; (2.25-ounce) green decorator sugar
- 1 cup Granulated sugar

Directions:

a) Place half the vanilla wafers in bowl of food processor fitted with knife blade. Process to fine crumbs. Remove crumbs and reserve. Repeat with remaining wafers.

b) Add pretzels (about 1 cup) to food processor and process to fine crumbs to make ½ cup crumbs.

c) In a large bowl, combine wafer crumbs, pretzel crumbs, powdered sugar, margarita concentrate, and cream cheese in a large bowl. Add tequila and Triple Sec, if desired. Stir until blended. Divide mixture in half. Wrap each half tightly in plastic and set aside.

d) Combine half the grated lime with decorator sugar and half with granulated sugar on small saucers or in small bowls, stirring to distribute lime peel evenly.

e) Remove plastic from 1 portion of the dough and shape into 1-inch balls.

f) After shaping each ball, roll each in green or white sugar. Work quickly, because balls dry quickly. Repeat until all dough is used.

g) Store in an airtight container in refrigerator up to 1 week

47. Margarita muffins

Yield: 12 Servings

Ingredient

- 2½ cup All-purpose flour
- ⅓ cup Granulated sugar
- 2 teaspoons Baking powder
- 1 teaspoon Baking soda
- 2 large Eggs
- 1 tablespoon Gold tequila
- 1 tablespoon Triple Sec
- 2 tablespoons Freshly squeezed lime juice
- 1 cup Buttermilk
- 1 tablespoon Lemon zest
- 2 teaspoons Lime zest
- Kosher salt

Directions:

a) Preheat the oven to 400. Whisk or sift together flour, sugar, baking powder, and baking soda in a large bowl. In a medium bowl, lightly beat the eggs. Add remaining wet Ingredients and mix well.

b) Make a well in the center of the dry Ingredients. Add liquids, lemon zest, and lime zest. Stir gently just to blend the wet and dry mixture. Spoon into greased muffin containers. Sprinkle kosher salt lightly over tops of muffins. Bake 15 to 20 minutes. Remove from pan and cool on rack.

48. Margarita pork kabobs

Yield: 1 Servings

Ingredient

- 1 pounds Armour Trim and Tender Pork Tenderloin, cut into 1 inch cubes
- 1 cup Margarita mix (OR 1 cup lime juice, 4 t. sugar, 1/2 t. salt)
- 1 teaspoon Ground coriander
- 1 Clove garlic; minced
- 1 large Green or red pepper; cut into 8 pieces
- 2 tablespoons Butter; softened
- 2 Ears corn; cut into 8 pieces
- 2 teaspoons Lime juice
- $\frac{1}{8}$ teaspoon Sugar
- 1 tablespoon Minced parsley

Directions:

a) Combine margarita mix, coriander, and garlic. Place pork cubes in heavy plastic bag; pour marinade over to cover. Marinate for at least 30 minutes.

b) Blend together well the butter, lime juice, sugar, and parsley; set aside.

c) Thread pork cubes onto skewers, alternating with pieces of corn and pepper.

d) Grill over hot coals, basting with butter mixture, for 10-15 minutes, turning frequently.

49. Margarita shrimp and vegetable kabobs

Yield: 1 servings

Ingredient

- 1 Envelope Good Seasons Italian Salad Dressing Mix
- ½ cup Oil
- ¼ cup Tequila
- ¼ cup Lime juice
- 1 pounds Large shrimp; cleaned
- Assorted cut-up fresh vegetables;
- Lime slices
- Edible fresh flower

Directions:

a) Mix salad dressing mix, oil, tequila and lime juice until well blended.

b) Pour over shrimp and vegetables; cover. Refrigerate 1 hour or overnight to marinate. Drain. Arrange shrimp and vegetables on skewers. Grill kabobs on grill over medium-hot coals 10 to 15 minutes, turning once. Garnish with lime slices and edible fresh flower.

50. Margarita shrimp skewers

Yield: 27 Servings

Ingredient

- ½ cup Tequila
- ¼ cup Fresh lime juice
- 1½ ounce Orange juice concentrate; thawed
- 2 teaspoons Vegetable oil
- 1½ pounds Medium shrimp; peeled and deveined
- Soaked bamboo skewers
- 3 Fresh jalapenos; cut as directed
- 1 large Red bell pepper; cut into 1/2-inch squares
- Coarse salt
- Minced fresh cilantro
- Lime wedges

Directions:

a) CUT each jalapeno into 8 small pieces Prepare marinade, combining Ingredients in a small bowl. Place shrimp in a plastic bag or shallow dish, pour marinade over them and refrigerate for 30 minutes.

b) Fire up grill, bringing temperature to high (1 to 2 seconds with the hand test).

c) While grill heats, drain shrimp, discarding marinade. Skewer shrimp with jalapenos and bell pepper pieces, avoiding crowing. Slide one end of the first shrimp on a skewer, add a piece of jalapeno and bell pepper to rest in the curve of the shrimp, and then slide the other end of the shrimp over the skewer. Repeat on the same skewer with a second shrimp and the jalapeno and bell pepper pieces. Assemble remaining kebabs and sprinkle them lightly with salt.

d) Grill kebabs uncovered over high heat for $1\frac{1}{2}$ to 2 minutes per side, until shrimp are just opaque with lightly browned edges. The jalapeno and bell pepper should remain a bit crisp. If grilling covered, cook kebabs the same amount of time, turning once midway.

e) When done, sprinkle kebabs lightly with cilantro and serve them hot, with lime wedges for squeezing.

51. Margarita shrimp tacos

Yield: 6 Servings

Ingredient

- 1½ pounds Shell-on Shrimp; uncooked
- ½ cup Tequila
- ½ cup Lime juice
- 1 teaspoon Salt
- 1 Clove minced Garlic clove; or more to taste
- 3 tablespoons Olive oil; or less
- 2 tablespoons Chopped cilantro
- 24 Flour tortillas; (6 or 7 inches)
- Shredded lettuce
- 1 Avocado; sliced; or more
- Salsa fresca; as needed
- 1 can (15 oz.) Black beans
- 1 can (10 oz.) Corn kernels

- ½ cup Chopped red onion
- ¼ cup Olive oil
- 2 tablespoons Lime juice
- ¼ teaspoon Ground cumin
- ¼ teaspoon Oregano
- ¼ teaspoon Salt

Directions:

a) Peel and devein shrimp, retaining tails, if desired; set aside. Combine tequila, lime juice, salt; pour over shrimp and marinate no more than 1 hour.

b) Sauté minced garlic in 1 tablespoon oil until light brown; add shrimp, cook and stir until done, 2 to 3 minutes. Add oil as needed.

c) Sprinkle with cilantro and keep warm. For each taco, fold 2 soft tortillas together; fill with shredded lettuce and Black Bean and Corn Relish. Top with shrimp, avocado slices and salsa.

d) Black Bean and Corn Relish: Rinse and drain beans; drain corn, combine beans and corn with remaining Ingredients; refrigerate to blend flavors.

52. Fajitas served with a tequila sunrise

Yield: 2 servings

Ingredient

- 1 tablespoon Vegetable oil
- 1 small Onion; finely chopped
- 2 Garlic cloves
- 1 Red chili; finely chopped
- 1 teaspoon Ground cumin
- 1 400 grams can red kidney beans; drained and rinsed
- 1 Lime
- 1 tablespoon Vegetable oil
- 1 small Red pepper; deseeded
- 1 small Yellow pepper
- 2 large Green chillies; sliced
- 1 Red onion
- 1 small Bunch coriander

- Salt and pepper
- 150 millilitres Sour cream
- 100 grams Cheddar cheese; grated
- 4 Flour tortillas
- 120 millilitres Tequila
- 175 millilitres Orange juice
- 2 tablespoons Grenadine syrup
- Ice; to serve
- 1 Lime; cut into wedges to garnish
- 1 Jar ready-made salsa
- 1 Bag green salad leaves

Directions:

a) For the Refried Beans: Heat a small pan with 1 Tablespoons vegetable oil. Stir in the chopped onion and fry for a minute.

b) Crush in the garlic cloves and add 1 teaspoons ground cumin and chopped red chilli. Cook for 2-3 minutes until softened.

c) For the Vegetable Filling: Start by heating a griddle pan until very hot, and almost smoking. Add 1 Tablespoons oil to the pan.

d) Chop the red pepper into strips and add to the pan along with the yellow pepper strips. Cook for 3-4 minutes until slightly charred.

e) Slice up the onion into eight wedges and add to the softened peppers, along with the green chilli strips. Cook for 2-3 minutes until charred, turning occasionally.

f) Add the red kidney beans to the softened onion mixture and squeeze in the juice from 1 lime. Cook for another 3-4 minutes, until softened. Chop the coriander, leaving a couple of sprigs to garnish.

g) Cook the flour tortillas on high in the microwave for 30 seconds. Take the beans off the heat and mash the mix to a chunky puree with a potato masher. Add the chopped coriander and season.

h) Take the flour tortillas and add some of the refried beans onto each. Top with the vegetables, a drizzle of sour cream and a sprinkling of cheese.

i) Roll up and place seam side down on the serving plate. Garnish with the coriander, salsa and mixed leaves.

j) For the Tequila Sunrise: Mix the tequila and orange juice in a measuring jug. Pour over a glass filled with ice. Tilt the glass slightly and spoon in the grenadine syrup. Drop in a lime wedge as garnish and serve with the fajitas.

53. Gala nachos with mango-tequila sauce

Yield: 6 servings

Ingredient

- 6 Corn OR 4 Flour tortillas
- 3 tablespoons Butter
- 6 tablespoons Sugar up to
- 1½ quart Ice cream or sherbet or a mixture
- 3 cups Cut fresh fruit
- Mango-Tequila Sauce;
- Sugared Nuts
- ¾ cup Chocolate chips

Directions:

a) Stack the tortillas in one pile and cut into triangles, 6 each for corn, or 8 each for flour.

b) Place ½ tablespoon of the butter and 1 tablespoon of the sugar in a large frying pan. Set over medium heat until the butter foams and the sugar melts.

c) Add as many tortilla triangles as will fit without overlapping and fry until they puff up, about 1 minute. Turn and fry on the other side until golden, about 1 minute more. Remove to a plate without overlapping. Add more butter and sugar to the pan and continue more rounds until all of the triangles are crisped.

d) To assemble, arrange scoops of ice cream or sherbet in the center of a large platter. Strew fruit pieces around the ice cream and tuck tortilla triangles in here and there. Spoon Mango-Tequila sauce over all. Dot with Sugared Nuts and chocolate chips. Serve right away.

54. Lime and tequila sweet potatoes

Yield: 1 servings

Ingredient

- 2 pounds Sweet potatoes; peeled
- $\frac{1}{4}$ cup Fresh lime juice
- 2 tablespoons Honey
- 1 tablespoon Tequila

Directions:

a) Cut sweet potatoes into $\frac{3}{4}$ inch thick slices. Boil slices in a large pan on high heat for about 6 minutes. Drain. Sweet potatoes should be just tender. In a bowl mix together lime juice, honey and tequila.

b) Brush over potatoes. Grill on greased grate for 4 to 6 minutes. Brush repeatedly with mixture and turn frequently. Sweet potatoes are done when they are browned.

55. Grilled tequila lime pineapple chunks

Yield: 4 servings

Ingredient

- 1 large Ripe pineapple
- ¼ cup Tequila
- ¼ cup Freshly squeezed lime juice
- 2 tablespoons Brown sugar

Directions:

a) In a medium bowl, combine tequila, lime juice and sugar. Add pineapple chunks and toss to coat. Let marinate 30 minutes at room temperature

b) Preheat grill to medium high. Drain pineapple chunks and divide among skewers. Brush grill well, wipe with oiled paper towel and place skewers on grill at an angle.

c) Cook a total of 68 minutes, turning frequently, until outside is lightly caramelized.

d) Remove from grill, let cool slightly and serve 2 skewers in each bowl of Watermelon Granita.

CLASSIC MARGARITA COCKTAILS

56. Apricot margaritas

Yield: 16 Servings

Ingredients

- 46 ounces Apricot nectar
- 6 ounces Frozen lemonade concentrate; Thawed
- 1 cup Tequila
- ½ cup Apricot brandy
- 4 cups Crushed ice
- Apricot or lemon slices; Optional
- Coarse salt; optional

Directions

a) In 4-quart non metal container, combine apricot nectar, lemonade concentrate, tequila, brandy and ice. Cover; freeze about 4 hours or until of slush consistency, stirring occasionally.

b) At serving time, stir mixture. Spoon 3 cups mixture at a time into blender container. Cover; blend until of desired consistency.

c) To serve, rub rims of glasses with lemon slices; dip rims in coarse salt. Fill each glass with margarita mixture. Garnish with apricot slices.

57. Beer margarita

Yield: 1 Serving

Ingredient

- 6 ounces Can frozen concentrated Limeade
- 6-ounce Tequila
- 6-ounce Beer

Directions

a) Combine Ingredients in blender, add a couple of ice cubes and blend briefly. Allow to set for a few minutes.

b) Pour contents over ice in salt rimmed glass.

58.   Blue margarita

Yield: 1 servings

Ingredient

- 1½ fluid ounce Tequila
- 1 fluid ounce Lime juice
- ½ fluid ounce Blue Curacao

Directions

a) Rub rim of glass with lime juice and dip in bar salt.

b) Shake Ingredients with ice and strain into margarita glass.

59. Cactus pear margaritas

Yield: 4 servings

Ingredient

- Lime wedge
- Coarse salt
- 8 ounces White tequila
- 4 ounces Cointreau
- 4 ounces Cactus pear juice
- 2 ounces Roses lime juice
- 2 cups Ice cubes

Directions

a) Rub lime wedge around the rim of cocktail glasses and dip the rim into a saucer of coarse salt.

b) Place tequila, Cointreau, cactus pear and lime juice and ice cubes in a blender and blend until frothy.

c) Divide among glasses.

60. Cafe margaritas

Yield: 12 Servings

Ingredient

- Lime wedges
- Coarse salt
- 3½ cup Homemade Sweet and Sour Mix
- 1 cup Gold tequila
- ½ cup Triple sec
- 16 Ice cubes
- 12 Lime slices

Directions

a) Rub rims of 12 glasses with lime wedges. Dip rims in coarse salt.

b) Combine 1-¾ cups sweet and sour mix, ½ cup tequila, ¼ cup triple sec and 8 ice cubes in blender. Process until well blended. Pour into 6 glasses.

c) Repeat with remaining sweet and sour mix, tequila, triple sec and ice cubes. Pour into 6 glasses. Garnish with lime slice.

61. Fresh lime margaritas

Yield: 4 Servings

Ingredient

- 1 cup Fresh lime juice
- Salt
- 1 cup Cuervo Gold tequila
- ½ cup Triple Sec orange liqueur
- 1 tablespoon Sugar
- 1 tablespoon Water
- 1 Egg white
- 1 quart Crushed ice

Directions

a) Moisten the rims of 4 (7-oz.) glasses with a little lime juice. Roll the rims in salt to coat. Refrigerate.

b) Mix the sugar with the water. Place in a blender with the tequila, lime juice, triple sec, and egg white. Blend well; add the crushed ice and blend briefly.

c) Pour carefully into the glasses without washing off any of the salt. Add more ice to taste if the drink is too strong.

62. Frothy margarita

Yield: 1 Servings

Ingredient

- Lime juice
- Salt
- 1½ ounce Tequila
- ½ ounce Orange liqueur
- 3 tablespoons Bottled sweet and sour mix
- Crushed ice

Directions

a) Moisten rim of glass with lime juice and swirl glass rim in mound of salt to coat edge.

b) Combine tequila, orange liqueur and sweet and sour mix with crushed ice in blender.

c) Blend until frothy and pour into prepared glass.

63. Frozen mango margarita

Yield: 4 Servings

Ingredient

- ½ cup Sugar
- ½ cup Water
- 1 Piece Fresh ginger - (1" long); sliced
- 2 medium Mangoes; peeled, pitted
- ½ cup Vodka
- 2 cup Ice cubes

Directions

a) Combine the sugar, water and ginger in heavy small saucepan. Stir over medium heat until sugar dissolves. Simmer 5 minutes. Remove from heat.

b) Cover and let steep 1 hour. Strain. Puree mangoes in a blender.

c) Pour into measuring cup. Return ¾ cup puree to blender. Add ½ cup ginger syrup, vodka and ice cubes to blender. Blend until smooth.

d) Serve in martini glasses.

64.   Frozen melon margaritas

Yield: 4 servings

Ingredient

- 3½ cup Honeydew melon balls
- ¾ cup Tequila; white
- ⅓ cup Fresh lime juice
- ¼ cup Sugar; or to taste

Directions

a) Remove and discard rind and seeds from melon and cut enough fruit into ½ inch cubes to measure 3½ cups.

b) Freeze melon cubes in a sealable plastic bag at least 3 hours and up to a week.

c) Puree frozen melon cubes in a blender with remaining Ingredients until smooth. Pour drink into 4 stemmed glasses.

65.   Jalapeno margaritas

Yield: 1 Servings

Ingredient

- 4 Jalapeno peppers, halved lengthways
- 16 ounces tequila
- 1-ounce Triple Sec liqueur
- 3 ounces bottled/fresh lime juice
- Coarse salt to garnish (optional)

Directions

a) Put the peppers into the bottle of tequila and allow to steep for at least three days. For 4 margaritas, pour 150ml ($\frac{1}{4}$ pint) of jalapeno tequila, 30ml of Triple Sec and 90ml of lime juice into a cocktail shaker filled with ice.

b) Stir and strain into glasses over fresh ice cubes.

66.   Margarita granita

Yield: 4 Servings

Ingredients

- 1 cup plus 2 tablespoons sugar
- 1 tablespoon finely grated lime zest
- 6 tablespoons freshly squeezed lime juice (about 3 limes)
- 3 tablespoons tequila
- 2 tablespoons fresh orange juice
- Coarse salt
- Lime wedges, for serving (optional)

Directions

a) In a medium saucepan, cook 3 3/4 cups water and sugar over medium-high heat, stirring, until sugar has dissolved, about 1 minute. Stir in lime zest and juice, tequila, and orange juice. Season with 1/4 teaspoon salt.

b) Pour mixture into a shallow dish; cool, then cover tightly with plastic wrap. Freeze until set, 6 hours or overnight. Using the tines of a fork, scrape mixture until flakes form. Freeze (covered) until ready to serve.

c) Garnish with lime wedges, if desired.

67. Papaya margarita

Yield: 12 servings

Ingredient

- 2 Papayas, peeled and chopped
- 1 cup Gold tequila
- ¾ cup Triple Sec
- ½ cup Fresh lime juice plus 2
- TB
- Crushed ice
- Salt for the rim of the
- Glass
- 4 slices Star fruit

Directions

a) In a food processor, puree the papaya until smooth. Using a rubber spatula, remove and place in a small container. Refrigerate for 1 hour.

b) In a blender, add half of the puree, half of the tequila, $\frac{1}{4}$ cup lime juice and fill with crushed ice. Blend the mixture on high until thick and slushy. Pour into a pitcher.

c) Repeat with the remaining Ingredients. Place the rim of the glass in the 2 tablespoons of lime juice and then in the salt.

d) Pour into the glasses and garnish with a piece of star fruit on the rim.

68. Raspberry margarita

Yield: 1 Servings

Ingredient

- 1 pack (small) frozen raspberries; 6 ounces
- 1 can (6-oz.) frozen limeade
- 1 Can tequila or rum
- 2 ounces Triple sec

Directions

a) Put all Ingredients in a blender.

b) Blend, adding water for desired consistency. Serves 6 to 8.

69. Watermelon margarita

Yield: 1 Servings

Ingredient

- 4 cups Fresh watermelon juice
- 1 cup Lime juice
- ½ cup Cointreau
- ½ cup Tequila; up to 1 cup

Directions

a) Mix together and pour over ice.

70. Yucatin margaritas with fruit

Yield: 12 Servings

Ingredient

- Lime wedges
- Sugar
- 3 cups Homemade Sweet and Sour Mix
- 1 cup Gold tequila
- 12 tablespoons Papaya nectar
- 12 tablespoons Guava nectar
- $\frac{1}{2}$ cup Canned cream of coconut
- 16 Ice cubes
- 12 Lime slices
- Rub rims of 12 glasses with lime wedges. Dip rims in sugar.

Directions

a) Combine 1-$\frac{1}{2}$ cups sweet and sour mix, $\frac{1}{2}$ cup tequila, 6 tablespoons papaya nectar, 6 tablespoons guava nectar, $\frac{1}{4}$ cup cream of coconut and 8 ice cubes in blender. Process until blended. Pour into 6 glasses.

b) Repeat with remaining sweet and sour mix, tequila, both nectars, cream of coconut and ice cubes. Pour into 6 glasses.

c) Garnish each with lime slice.

71.   Beer margarita

Yield: 1 Serving

Ingredient

- 6 ounce Can frozen concentrated Limeade
- 6-ounce Tequila
- 6-ounce Beer

Directions

a) Combine Ingredients in blender, add a couple of ice cubes and blend briefly. Allow to set for a few minutes.

b) Pour contents over ice in salt rimmed glass.

72. Margarita liqueur

Ingredient

- 1 Bottle silver tequila
- 1 Peel of orange; cut in continuous spiral
- 1 Peel of lime; cut in continuous spiral
- 6 ounces Cointreau

Directions

a) Add citrus peel to tequila in bottle, and then add the Cointreau to taste. Keep refrigerated and serve in sherry glasses.

b) Take a bottle of this to the host of a dinner party instead of a bottle of wine.

73. Iced margarita

Ingredient

- 1/2 cup gold tequila
- 1/2 cup fresh lime juice
- 1 to 2 Tablespoons fine salt
- 1 cup finely crushed ice
- 1 slice lime, halved

Directions

a) Put 2 margarita glasses in the freezer for at least 1 hour. Mix the tequila and lime juice and place in the freezer.
b) Put the salt onto a shallow plate. When ready to serve, dip the rim of the chilled glasses in the salt (because the glasses are cold, the salt will stick to the rim).
c) Fill the glasses with the crushed ice and then pour in the tequila-lime juice mixture. Serve immediately with the piece of lime.
d) Serves 2

74. Green Margarita

Ingredients

- Lime wedge, for rim of glass, plus lime slice, for garnish
- Coarse salt, for rim of glass
- 2 ounces Super Green Juice
- 2 ounces tequila
- 1-ounce orange liqueur, such as Cointreau

Super Green Juice:

- 1 to 2 large, juicy lemons, peel removed
- 1 medium Granny Smith apple, peeled
- 2 romaine leaves
- 1/2 large cucumber
- 1 cup loosely packed hearty greens, such as spinach or kale

Directions

a) Moisten the rim of a margarita glass with a wedge of lime, and then roll the glass at an angle in the salt so that only the outside of the glass is salted.

b) Combine the Super Green Juice, tequila and orange liqueur in a cocktail shaker filled with ice. Shake vigorously for 8 to 10 seconds. Strain into the prepared glass over ice. Garnish with a slice of lime.

c) **Super Green Juice:** Juice, in this order, the lemons, apple, romaine, cucumber and greens, following your juicer's specific settings for each. Serve the juice immediately over ice, if desired.

MODERN MARGARITA COCKTAILS

75. Casa Ginger Mint Paloma

Ingredients

- 2 oz. Casamigos Reposado
- 1.5 oz. grapefruit juice
- 1 oz. fresh lime juice
- .5 oz. simple syrup
- 8-10 mint leaves

Direction

a) Muddle herbs. Combine all Ingredients into tin shaker. Add ice. Shake vigorously for 8-10 seconds. Fine strain into highball glass. Add fresh ice.

b) Garnish with grapefruit wheel and mint sprig.

76.   Oaxacan Old Fashioned

Ingredients

- 1.5 oz. Corralejo Reposado Tequila
- .5 VIDA Mezcal
- 1 bar spoon agave nectar
- 2 dashes Angostura Bitters
- 2 dashes Bittermens Xocaloctl Bitters

Directions

a) Stir all Ingredients with ice and strain over a large format ice cube in a rocks glass.

b) Garnish with a long peel of an orange and its oils.

77.   The Marble Queen

Ingredients

- 1.5 oz. Tequila
- 1 oz. cream of coconut
- 0.5 oz. lime juice

Directions

a) Combine all Ingredients and shake over ice.

b) Serve with a salted or spiced rim.

78.   Milagro Mexican Martini

Ingredients

- 2 oz. Milagro Select Reposado
- 0.75 oz. vermouth bianco
- 1 dash orange bitters
- Lemon twist

Directions

a) Pour all Ingredients into a mixing glass, add ice and stir until cold.

b) Strain into a chilled cocktail coupe glass and garnish with a lemon twist.

79. El Gavilan

Ingredients

- 2 oz. Tress Agaves Reposado
- .5 oz. grapefruit juice
- .75 oz. lime juice
- .75 oz. simple syrup
- 1 dash Angostura Bitters
- Top with grapefruit soda

Directions

a) Add all Ingredients except soda in the shaker; add ice, shake and strain over ice.

b) Top off with Mexican soda and garnish with lime wheel.

80.   It's Greek to Me

Ingredients

- 4 slices ginger
- 1 oz. Tequila
- 0.5 oz. Mavrakis Tsipouro
- 1 oz. lime juice
- 0.75 oz. Chambord
- 0.5 oz. agave
- 1 dash Angostura bitters

Directions

a) Muddle ginger into the bottom of a shaker. Combine all other Ingredients in shaker over ice and shake.

b) Strain into a cocktail glass and garnish with sage.

81.   Blue-cumber Lime Margarita

Ingredients

- 1.5 oz. Blue Nectar Silver
- 3-4 slices of cucumber
- .75 oz. Cointreau
- 1.5 oz. lime juice
- 1.5 oz. lime simple syrup

Directions

a) Muddle cucumber with Blue Nectar Tequila. Add remaining Ingredients and shake over ice. Strain into rocks glass. Garnish with cucumber slice.

b) Lime Syrup: Combine 2 cups of water, 1.5 cups of sugar, and zest of 1 lime in a saucepan over medium heat until sugar dissolves. Remove from heat and cool until ready for use.

82.   Manhattan Goes Hollywood

Ingredients

- 3 oz. Casamigos Anejo Tequila
- 0.75 teaspoons maple syrup
- 4 dashes Orange Bitters

Directions

a) Add all Ingredients to mixing glass, add large ice, and stir thoroughly. Taste for balance and single strain into a rocks glass.

b) Garnish and serve.

83. The Mystic Marvel

Ingredients

- 1.5 oz. Casamigos Tequila
- 1 oz. prickly pear purée
- 0.75 oz. agave
- 0.75 oz. lime juice

Directions

a) Combine all Ingredients in a shaker over ice and shake.

b) Strain over fresh ice and garnish with a salt rim and lime.

84. Rosemary Margarita

Ingredients

- 2 oz. Herradura Blanco
- 1 oz. Rosemary-infused simple syrup
- 0.75 oz. fresh lemon juice
- 0.5 oz. store-bought pear puree
- Splash club soda

Directions

a) Add all Ingredients (except club soda) to cocktail shaker and shake to combine.

b) Pour into Collins glass, served on the rocks. Top with splash of club soda.

c) Garnish with fresh rosemary sprig.

85.   Baccarat Rouge

Ingredients

- 2 oz. Tequila
- 1 oz. Passion fruit juice
- 0.25 oz. Allspice Dram
- 0.25 oz. lime juice
- 0.25 oz. Cardamaro Amaro

Directions

a) Add all Ingredients to a shaker tin with ice and shake vigorously. Strain into a rocks glass with fresh ice.

b) Garnish with a candied hibiscus flower.

86.   Blood Orange Margarita

Ingredients

- 1.5 oz. Silver Tequila
- 0.5 oz. Cointreau
- 0.5 blood orange juice
- 0.75 oz. simple syrup
- 1 oz. lime juice

Directions

a) Fill a mixing tin with ice. Add all Ingredients and shake vigorously. Empty shaker contents into a rocks glass with a salted rim.

b) Garnish with a blood orange slice.

87.   Something Wicked

Ingredients

- 0.75 oz. Sangrita Mix
- 0.75 oz. lime juice
- 1.5 oz. pineapple juice
- 2 oz. Mezcal
- Smoked Salt
- 1 Lime

Directions

a) Line the rim of a glass with smoked salt by first coating with lime and rolling in salt. Pour all Ingredients in a shaker with ice and shake before straining into a glass with ice. Garnish with a slice of lime.

b) For the Sangrita: Blend half of a pineapple, 1 cucumber, 1 pint of blackberries, 5 ancho chilies, 1.5 cup lime juice, 1 cup orange juice, .5 cup pomegranate juice, and 1.5 cup sugar and strain.

c) Refrigerate and store for up to 2 weeks.

88. The Bluebonnet

Ingredients

- 1.5 oz. tequila blanco
- 1.5 oz. fresh lime juice
- .75 oz. Cointreau
- 1.5 oz. simple syrup
- A few drops blue curacao
- A few drops grenadine

Directions

a) Combine all Ingredients and shake with ice.

b) Pour over ice into a rocks glass and garnish with lemon wedge and jalapeno slice.

89. Tequila's New Fashion

Ingredients

- 2 oz. Casamigos Añejo
- .5 oz. simple syrup
- 2 dashes angostura bitters
- 2 dashes banana bitters

Directions

a) Add all Ingredients in mixing glass with ice.

b) Stir and strain into bucket glass over single ice block. Garnish with a bruleed plantain.

90. Ghost pepper margarita

Ingredients

- 2 oz. Avion Silver Tequila
- .5 oz. Grand Marnier
- .5 oz. lime juice
- .5 oz. lemon juice
- 1.5 oz. Ghost Chili Simple Syrup

Directions

a) Add all Ingredients together with ice in a cocktail shaker, shake and strain over fresh ice in a rocks glass that has a chili salt rim. Serve with a lime wheel and enjoy.

b) Ghost Chili Simple Syrup: Take 1 cup of water and 1 cup of brown demerara with one dried ghost chili pepper, bring to a boil and let cool.

91.   Mourning Doves

Ingredients

- 1.5 oz. El Jimador Reposado
- .5 oz. Amaro di Angostura
- .5 oz. maple syrup
- .5 oz. grapefruit juice
- .75 oz. lemon juice
- .25 oz. simple syrup

Directions

a) Mix all Ingredients and serve on the rocks.

b) Garnish with a lemon wheel.

92. Smokey Arroyo

Ingredients

- 1.5 oz. Sombra Mezcal
- 1 oz. grapefruit juice
- .5 oz. lime juice
- .5 oz. rosemary simple syrup
- Salt (if desired)

Directions

a) Combine Sombra, grapefruit juice, lime juice, and rosemary syrup in a shaker with ice, and shake vigorously. Salt the rim of a rocks glass. Strain cocktail over ice in rocks glass.

b) Garnish with grapefruit wedge and rosemary sprig.

93.   Tepache Kid

Ingredients

- 2 oz. Tres Agaves Añejo
- 1 oz. pineapple puree
- 1 oz. tamarind syrup (tamarind paste mixed with equal parts refined sugar and water)
- 2 dash angostura bitters

Directions

a) Pour all Ingredients into the shaker with ice; shake and strain on the rocks and garnish with pineapple wedge.

94. Smokin' Margarita

Ingredients

- 2 oz. Avion Blanco
- 0.5 oz. Buenbicho Mezcal
- 0.75 oz. lime juice
- 0.5 oz. agave nectar

Directions

a) Combine all Ingredients over ice, shake, and strain over fresh ice in rocks glass that has been rimmed with salt.

95. Vampiro

Ingredients

- 1.5 oz. Tres Agaves Tequila Reposado
- 5 oz. Sangrita
- .5 oz. lime juice
- Balance with grapefruit soda

Directions

a) Pour tequila into serving glass, then add the sangrita mix and top off with grapefruit soda; stir Ingredients together and garnish with grapefruit wheel.

96.   Chai Mezcalita

Ingredients

- Salt, pinch
- 1 oz. lime juice
- 0.75 oz. Chai Syrup
- 1.25 oz. Banhez Mezcal
- 0.75 oz. silver tequila of choice
- 2 whole star anise for garnish

Directions

a) Add all measured Ingredients. Fill shaker with ice. Shake very well. Fill rocks glass with ice and strain into glass. Garnish with anise to serve.

b) For the Chai syrup: Combine 1-quart water, 1 Tablespoons whole allspice berries, .5 Tablespoons whole cloves, 8 whole star anise, 3 inches' fresh ginger rough chopped, 1 Tablespoons whole black peppercorns, .5 Tablespoons whole cardamom, 8 cinnamon sticks, and .5

Tablespoons vanilla extract in a pot and boil.

c) Then allow to simmer for 20 minutes, remove from heat, add 6 black tea bags and steep for 15 minutes. Add .75-quart sugar. Can refrigerate for up to 6 weeks.

97.   Hibiscus Smash

Ingredients

- 2 oz. Santo Reposado
- 1 oz. Hibiscus Tea
- 0.5 oz. Agave
- 0.75 oz. Lime Juice
- 0.25 cup Fresh Cilantro Leaves with Tender Stems
- Ice

Directions

a) Brew Hibiscus tea and let cool. In a cocktail shaker with ice add tequila, hibiscus tea, agave, lime juice and fresh cilantro.

b) Shake for 30 seconds. Double strain into a cocktail glass filled with ice.

98.   Devil's Margarita

Ingredient

- 1 1/2 ounces blanco tequila
- 1-ounce lime juice, freshly squeezed
- 3/4-ounce simple syrup
- 1/2-ounce red wine
- Garnish: lime wheel

Directions

a) Add the tequila, lime juice and simple syrup to a cocktail shaker with ice and shake until well-chilled.

b) Strain into a cocktail glass.

c) Float the red wine on top by slowly pouring it over the back of a bar spoon so it pools on the surface of the drink.

d) Garnish with a lime wheel.

99. Bloody maria

Ingredient

- 1 1/2 ounces tequila
- 2 dashes Worcestershire sauce
- Sprinkle of salt
- Sprinkle of pepper
- Sprinkle of celery salt
- Tomato juice

Directions

a) Build tequila and Worcestershire sauce in a double old-fashioned glass.
b) Sprinkle salt, pepper, and celery salt.
c) Fill with tomato juice and ice.

100. Yucatin margaritas with fruit

Yield: 12 Servings

Ingredient

- Lime wedges
- Sugar
- 3 cups Homemade Sweet and Sour Mix
- 1 cup Gold tequila
- 12 tablespoons Papaya nectar
- 12 tablespoons Guava nectar
- ½ cup Canned cream of coconut
- 16 Ice cubes
- 12 Lime slices
- Rub rims of 12 glasses with lime wedges. Dip rims in sugar.

Directions

d) Combine 1-½ cups sweet and sour mix, ½ cup tequila, 6 tablespoons papaya nectar, 6 tablespoons guava nectar, ¼ cup cream of coconut and 8 ice cubes in blender. Process until blended. Pour into 6 glasses.

e) Repeat with remaining sweet and sour mix, tequila, both nectars, cream of coconut and ice cubes. Pour into 6 glasses.

f) Garnish each with lime slice.

CONCLUSION

A human taste bud has five different tastes: salty, sweet, bitter, sour and umami; the margarita nails four of those five: the salty rim of the glass, the sweetness of the agave, the bitterness of the tequila, and the sourness of the limes. So when you take a sip of a margarita with salt, you cut the bitterness of the lime and tequila, while heightening the sweetness and sourness.

Margaritas are what you pour for life's happiest moments! This simple concoction of tequila, lime, agave and orange liqueur has stolen our hearts. Whether you like yours infused in your dishes, frozen, on the rocks, salt, or no salt, sweet or spicy, the margarita will rise to the occasion!

www.ingramcontent.com/pod-product-compliance
Lightning Source LLC
Chambersburg PA
CBHW071809080526
44589CB00012B/730